R.L. 3.1
P+s. 0.5

	DATE DUE	03-06
MAR 0 4 2008		

CARNOTAURUS

A Buddy Book
by
Christy Devillier

ABDO
Publishing Company

VISIT US AT

www.abdopub.com

Published by ABDO Publishing Company, 4940 Viking Drive, Edina, Minnesota 55435. Copyright © 2004 by Abdo Consulting Group, Inc. International copyrights reserved in all countries. No part of this book may be reproduced in any form without written permission from the publisher.

Printed in the United States.

Edited by: Michael P. Goecke
Contributing Editor: Matt Ray
Graphic Design: Denise Esner, Maria Hosley
Image Research: Deborah Coldiron
Illustrations: Denise Esner, Maria Hosley
Photographs: Corel, Photodisc

Library of Congress Cataloging-in-Publication Data

Devillier, Christy, 1971-
    Carnotaurus/Christy Devillier.
       p. cm.
    Includes index.
    Summary: Describes the physical characteristics, habitat, and behavior of a big, heavy dinosaur with two horns on its head.
    ISBN 1-59197-536-0
    1. Carnotaurus—Juvenile literature. [1. Carnotaurus. 2. Dinosaurs.] I. Title.

QE862.S3D475 2004
567.912—dc22

                           2003057812

TABLE OF CONTENTS

The Carnotaurus was an odd-looking dinosaur. It had a short head and a horn above each eye. The Carnotaurus lived about 100 million years ago.

The Carnotaurus was a big dinosaur. It was about 25 feet (eight m) long. It weighed about 2,000 pounds (907 kg). That is as heavy as an adult bison.

Carnotaurus

KAR-no-TAR-us

HOW DID THEY MOVE?

Scientists believe the Carnotaurus could run fast. It moved around on two strong legs. It had three toes on each foot. Each toe had a claw. The Carnotaurus also had a long tail.

TAIL

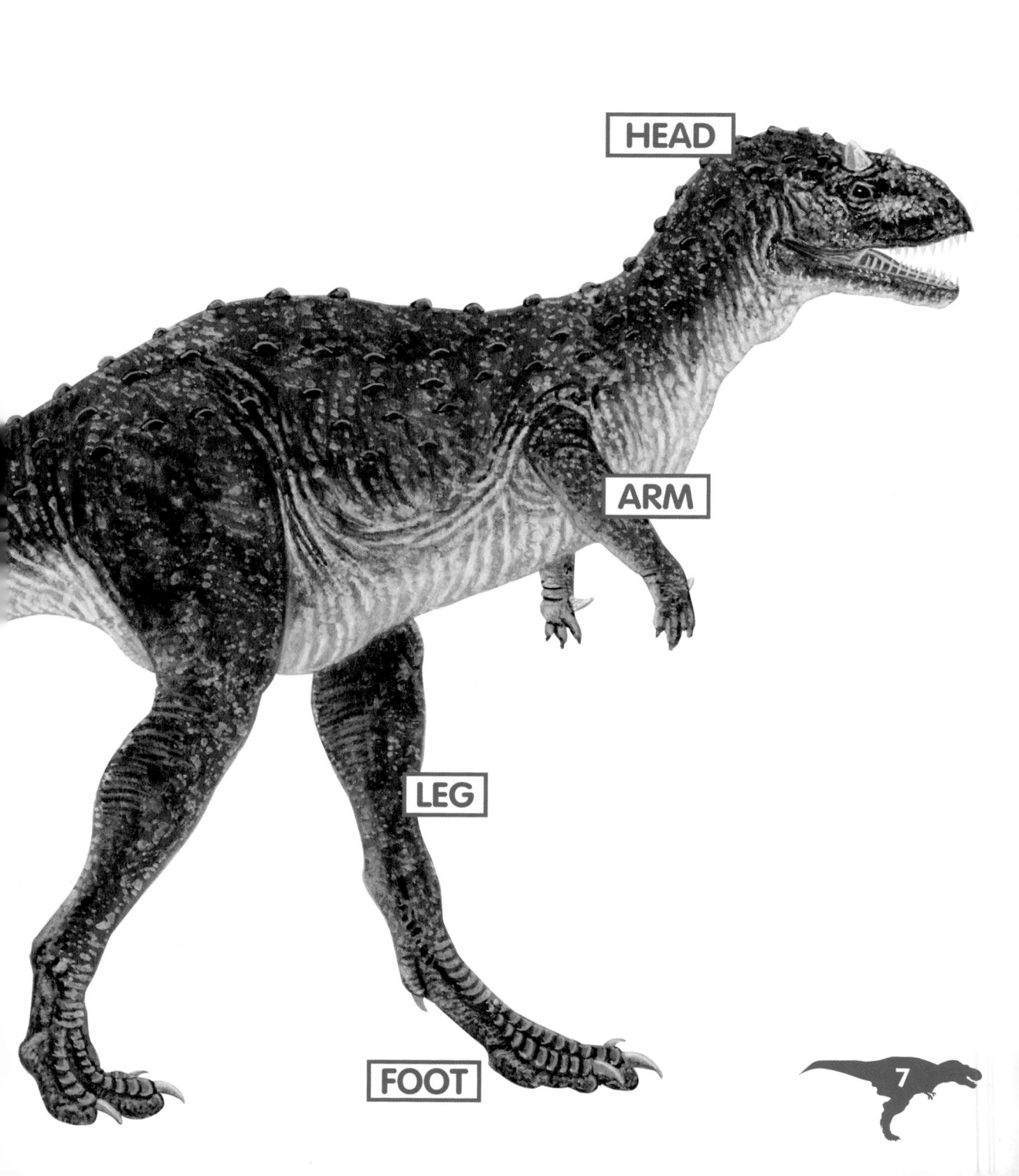

HEAD

ARM

LEG

FOOT

7

The Carnotaurus's arms were very short. They were probably weak. Scientists believe the Carnotaurus did not use its arms much.

The Carnotaurus had three clawed fingers on each hand. Each hand also had a spike. Scientists are not sure how the Carnotaurus used its hands.

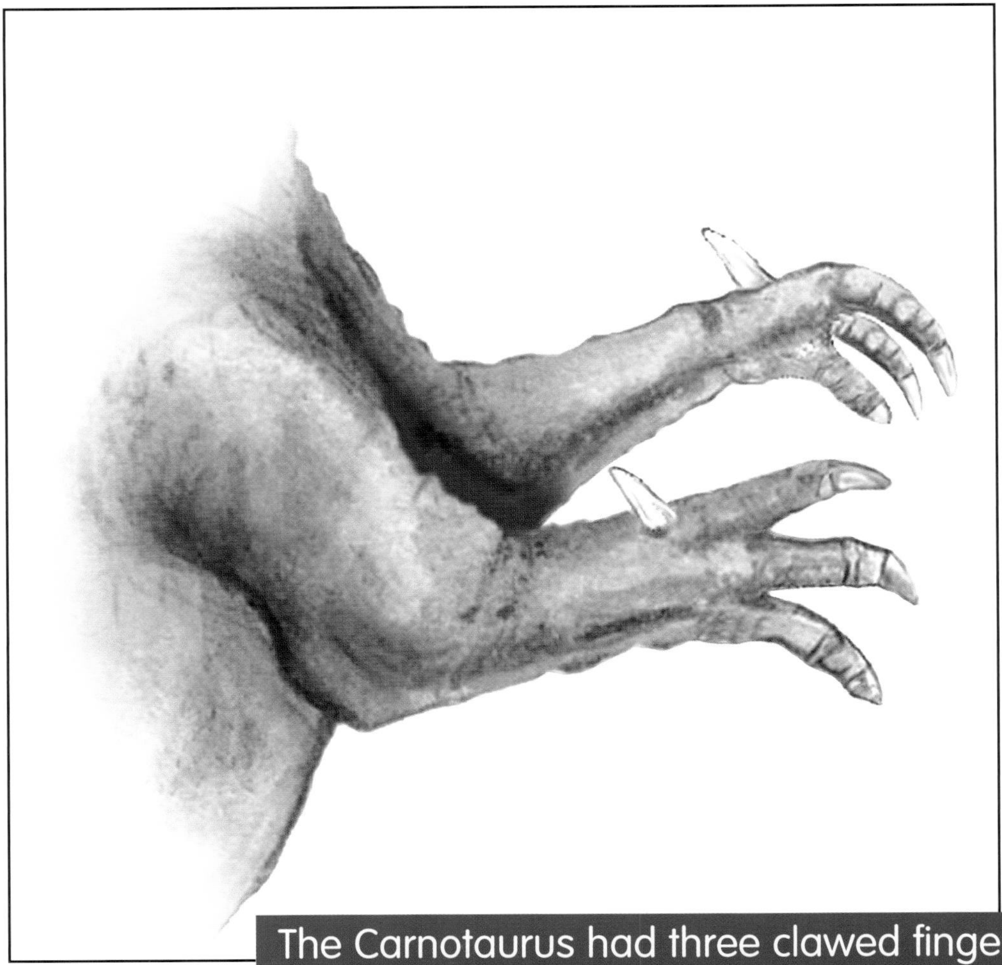

The Carnotaurus had three clawed fingers and a spike on each hand.

9

The Carnotaurus's name means "meat-eating bull." It is famous for its bull-like head.

The Carnotaurus also had special skin. Its skin had rows of bumps. Maybe these bumps were scales. Scales would make the Carnotaurus's skin very tough. Tough skin would help protect this dinosaur from bites and scratches.

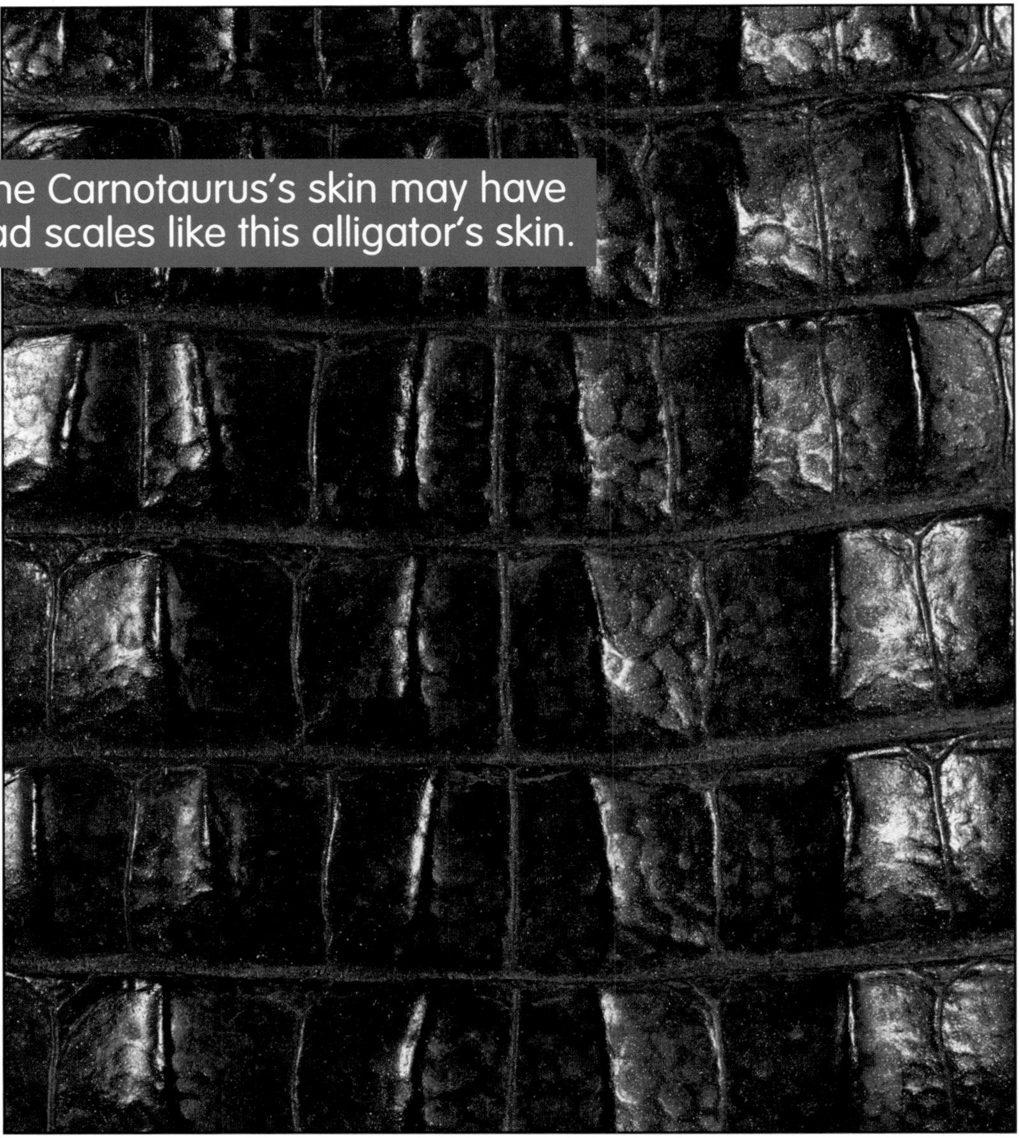

The Carnotaurus's skin may have had scales like this alligator's skin.

WHERE DID THEY LIVE?

The Carnotaurus lived in South America. It lived on land that is now Argentina.

The Carnotaurus lived about 100 million years ago. It lived during the Cretaceous period. This time period lasted about 79 million years.

The world's continents were in different places during the Cretaceous period.

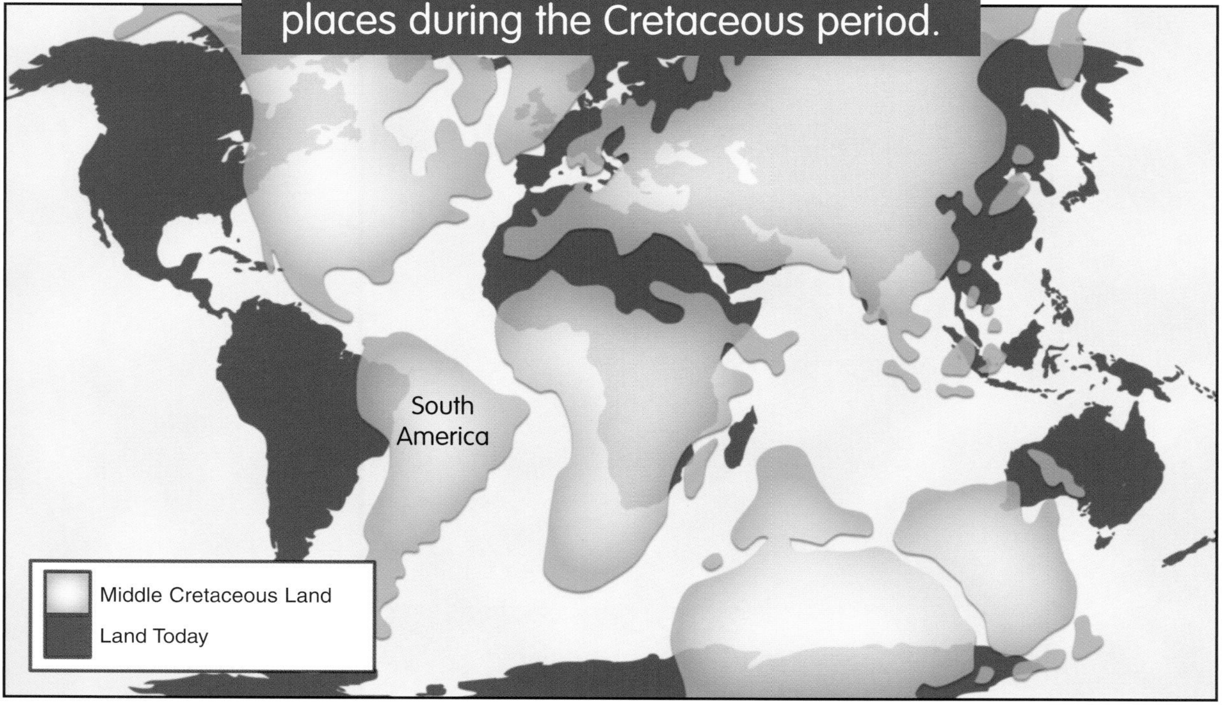

South America

Middle Cretaceous Land

Land Today

The world changed a lot during the Cretaceous period. The world's tropical weather began to cool. Seasons started happening. Continents broke apart and moved away from each other. More and more flowering plants grew in the forests.

All the dinosaurs died out 65 million years ago. This marked the end of the Cretaceous period.

Many kinds of flowering plants grew in the Cretaceous forests.

WHO ELSE LIVED THERE?

The Carnotaurus lived among insects, birds, and mammals. Fish, turtles, and plesiosaurs swam in the oceans.

The biggest plesiosaurs were 66 feet (20 m) long. These sea animals had flippers for swimming. They probably ate fish and other sea animals. All the plesiosaurs died out about 65 million years ago.

Plesiosaurs swam in the Cretaceous oceans.

There were other dinosaurs around, too. The Carnotaurus may have lived near the Giganotosaurus. Giganotosaurus means "giant southern reptile." It was bigger than the Tyrannosaurus rex.

The Giganotosaurus may have been the longest meat-eating dinosaur. It was about 45 feet (14 m) long. It weighed about 16,000 pounds (7,257 kg). Its huge mouth had sharp, eight-inch (20-cm) teeth.

The Giganotosaurus may have lived near the Carnotaurus.

WHAT DID THEY EAT?

The Carnotaurus was a carnivore. Carnivores eat meat. The Carnotaurus had sharp teeth and a strong bite for eating. Some scientists believe the Carnotaurus hunted small animals. Others believe it scavenged for food. Maybe the Carnotaurus was a hunter and a scavenger.

The Carnotaurus had sharp teeth and a strong bite.

Scientists believe the Carnotaurus had a keen sense of smell. The Carnotaurus may have had good eyesight, too. These skills would help it find food.

THE FAMILY TREE

The Carnotaurus was a theropod dinosaur. All theropod dinosaurs were meat-eaters. They walked on two legs. Other theropods were the Tyrannosaurus rex, the Giganotosaurus, and the Allosaurus.

The Allosaurus was bigger than the Carnotaurus. It was the biggest carnivore of the late Jurassic period. It lived about 150 million years ago in North America.

Three Theropod Dinosaurs

Tyrannosaurus Rex

Allosaurus

Carnotaurus

Some theropod dinosaurs had feathers. One was the Caudipteryx. It lived about 130 million years ago. The Caudipteryx was about the size of a turkey. Scientists believe it did not fly. Instead, the Caudipteryx ran on two long legs.

Does the feathered Caudipteryx prove that today's birds are related to dinosaurs? Many paleontologists say yes. Maybe dinosaurs did not die out. Maybe they slowly changed into other animals—birds!

The Caudipteryx was a dinosaur with feathers.

DISCOVERY

Dinosaur fossils have been found on every continent. Lately, people have been finding more and more fossils in South America. Bones from a Carnotaurus dinosaur were found in the Chubut province of Argentina. Dinosaur fossils have been found in Bolivia, Brazil, Chile, and Uruguay, too.

Paleontologists study fossils.

Paleontologists study fossils to learn about dinosaurs. José Bonaparte is a paleontologist. He has discovered many South American dinosaurs. Bonaparte was the first to discover the Carnotaurus. He named the Carnotaurus in 1985.

27

**Natural History Museum
of Los Angeles County**
900 Exposition Blvd.
Los Angeles, CA 90007
http://www.nhm.org/

Natural Science Museum
Madrid, Spain
Paseo de la Castellana
84, Madrid

Argentina Museum of Natural Science
Buenos Aires, Argentina

CARNOTAURUS

NAME MEANS	Meat-eating bull
DIET	Meat
WEIGHT	2,000 pounds (907 kg)
LENGTH	25 feet (8 m)
TIME	Middle Cretaceous Period
ANOTHER THEROPOD	Allosaurus
SPECIAL FEATURE	Bull-like head and tough skin
FOSSILS FOUND	Argentina

The Carnotaurus lived 100 million years ago.

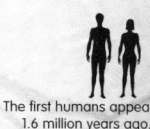

The first humans appeared 1.6 million years ago.

Triassic Period	Jurassic Period	Cretaceous Period	Tertiary Period
245 Million years ago	208 Million years ago	144 Million years ago	65 Million years ago
Mesozoic Era			Cenozoic Era

WEB SITES

To learn more about the Carnotaurus, visit ABDO Publishing Company on the World Wide Web. Web sites about the Carnotaurus are featured on our "Book Links" page. These links are routinely monitored and updated to provide the most current information available.

www.abdopub.com

IMPORTANT WORDS

carnivore a meat-eater.

continent one of the earth's seven main land areas.

Cretaceous period a period of time that happened 144–65 million years ago.

dinosaur reptiles that lived on land 248–65 million years ago.

fossil remains of very old animals and plants commonly found in the ground. A fossil can be a bone, a footprint, or any trace of life.

mammal most living things that belong to this special group have hair, give birth to live babies, and make milk to feed their babies.

paleontologist someone who studies very old life, such as dinosaurs, mostly by studying fossils.

scavengers animals that eat animals they did not kill.

tropical weather that is warm and wet.

INDEX